MANifesto:

**A Call for Men
to Become Warriors
for Kindness**

MANifesto
Copyright © 2020 Richard Matzkin

ISBN 978-1506-909-14-1 PBK

LCCN 2020908023

June 2020

Design by Riley K. Smith
Published and Distributed by
First Edition Design Publishing, Inc.
P.O. Box 17646, Sarasota, FL 34276-3217
www.firsteditiondesignpublishing.com

ALSO BY RICHARD MATZKIN:

THE ART OF AGING
Celebrating the Authentic Aging Self

LOVING PROMISES
The Master Class for Creating Magnificent
Relationship

ALSO BY RILEY K. SMITH:

MANACHAR AND MUNICHAR,
Two Celtic Tales

HOW TO BE A COUPLE AND STILL BE FREE

TRUE PARTNERS,
A workbook for building a lasting intimate
relationship

ONE TRUTH THAT CHANGES EVERYTHING

DEDICATION

I would like to dedicate
this book to Riley . . .
Courage, Wisdom, Love and Vision.
And, of course, to Alice.

Grateful thanks to Sandra Beddor,
Robbie Long, Pianta, and
Swami Muktananda.

RICHARD MATZKIN

I would like to dedicate this book to my
beloveds – my wife, Rhoda, extended family
and dear friends. . . and to
Richard for his wisdom and his friendship.
And, of course, to Alice.

Thanks to my compatriots and fellow travelers
on this journey of being human.

RILEY K. SMITH

MANifesto:

A Call for Men
to Become Warriors
for Kindness

Richard Matzkin, MA

Illustrations and design by
Riley K. Smith

INTRODUCTION

The motivation for me to write this poetic essay, this call to action for men, was my coming to realization of a truth that has been hiding in plain sight. I had been blind.

The news media is filled with reports of mass shootings, child molestation, road rage, vandalism, sexual harassment and domestic violence. We instinctively assume that men are the likely perpetrators ... and in the vast majority of cases ... they are. The incidence of war, rape, crime, torture, genocide, and terrorism are mostly at the hands of men. Though women are certainly not blameless, the reality is that *far greater amounts of the evil, hurtful and unloving actions in the world are committed by men — men who are not in touch with their heart.*

It's time we men open our eyes, realize our responsibility and do something about it. By maintaining silence in the face of malicious actions and not protesting, we are colluding. By not doing all we can to open ourselves to love, we remain part of the problem.

These are the dual goals of the book. First, to help men cultivate and develop their natural inclination, which is to love and be loved. And second, to apply their loving nature in support of efforts to heal the conflicts that divide person from person, community from community, and country from country.

Exhorting men to take action to address the wrongful activities of others and to open our hearts to love shouldn't be women's responsibility. We *are* our brother's keeper. It is necessary, and far more persuasive, if we, not women, are the ones to demand that our gender assume accountability for the pain we are causing. After all, we males are the main ones responsible for creating this mess — we should stop ignoring it and start cleaning it up.

The causes of men's aggression and violence are numerous and complex. The theme that seems to run through it all is that, generally speaking, we men find it difficult to get in touch with the loving part of ourselves. It's not that we can't love, we just tend to have more barriers to loving than women: a greater amount of testosterone, a deficiency of maternal instinct, a larger, more muscular physique, having more control of the reins of power, taking on the traditional role as protector of home and country, growing up in an environment of family, peer and societal conditioning that equates war with manhood and shames boys for being "sissies." All these factors and more make it so we men have to work harder at love.

This little book asks the men who read it to go beyond those barriers to loving, define what we deeply value and step up to the plate to take action. The book encourages us to dig deep and take on the life-changing work of opening our heart. It is not anti-male at all . . . it is pro-humanity, pro-love.

Humanity is at the edge of a precipice.

Rising totalitarian regimes, economic inequality, pervasive corruption and environmental destruction are rampant. Hate and greed are ascending. Kindness, sharing and cooperation are in eclipse. The world needs our love.

Opening to love, we become more loving and lovable human beings and that will be a step toward making our world a more loving and lovable place to live.

Richard Matzkin
Ojai, California
4/15/2020

HOW TO USE THE BOOK

Even though it can be easily done, MANifesto is not a book to read from cover-to-cover in one sitting. It is a book to be lived with. Don't rush through. Carefully read. Listen to your thoughts. Give yourself time to reflect. Put it down, pick it up later. Contained herein are seeds for a lifetime of contemplation of life and love.

The ideas are extremely condensed. Thoughts contained in the space of a few sentences or a paragraph might take a whole book to fully explain. Even one sentence can potentially open an inquiry that stimulates a whole new line of thought for you. There are wise gems here, but they need to be dug up, cleaned off, and carefully examined.

I suggest you read and reread the passages, especially those that resonate for you. Take your time. Share your thoughts with others. See how the ideas might apply to yourself. Think about how you might translate thought to action in your own life.

Compassionate action is the goal. MANifesto is about generating change. May the words of this book strike a chord that will reverberate with kindness and good will, in your heart and in the world.

{ MANIFESTO }

MEN . . . .

Men of good will.
We are being called to attention.

Our strong arms,
clear voice,
firm judgement and
dependable presence
are sorely needed now.

Our world is suffering. That suffering is
caused mostly by men among us
whose hearts are closed to love,
whose minds are closed to other's pain,
whose hands are closed to giving.

Open-hearted,
open-minded,
open handed men
are needed
more than ever.

Now is the time for us to assert our innate loving nature—

our benevolent,

strong,

incorruptible,

masculine

love.

That powerful love of ours is needed
to confront closed-hearted men,
who care only about themselves and use
lies, manipulation and intimidation to
enforce their greed for profit and control.

These are men who know the price of
everything . . .

and the value of nothing.

These are men that don't know how to
love.

Much of our lives we have looked to our women - mothers, wives and girlfriends to be the main providers of love in our family and relationships.

No more!

We have available a deep well of love inside us.

It is time for us to draw from that well.

Our beloved partner,
our precious children,
our family,
our friends,
our neighbors,
our country —
all are crying out
for us to reveal
that righteous,
powerful love
we know
we have
within us
to share . . .

not half-assed, dainty, pink valentine love,
but brawny, lusty love, love from
  our hearts,
   our guts,
    our bones,
     our balls.

Consider this simple, no-frills definition of love.

Love is extending care.
It is your desire for the well-being of those you love, and your willingness to spend your time, energy and resources in order to make this happen.

This is Real Love — committed, protective, supportive, affirming . . .

This is *love-in-action* . . . not merely
  the sentiments we feel
    the thoughts we think
      the words we speak.
Real Love is active — it is what we DO in our relationships.
It is the way we treat those we care about.

This is the kind of love a man can feel good about.

No need to be somebody special,
a philosopher, genius or holy man.
Instinctively, we already know what we
need to know about love.

We know these truths about love.

We know
that the power of love is
mind-blowing . . .
soul-stirring . . .
life-altering . . .
world-changing.

We know
that love is the greatest gift we can give
and the most precious gift we can receive.

We know
that love is an essential ingredient
for a fulfilling life.
Every living being needs to love and
be loved in order to survive and thrive.

We know
that all the money, knowledge, fame
and possessions we acquire are worthless,
unless we have love in our life.

We know
that life is a school whose curriculum is to
teach love.
Everyone in our life —
our parents,
our children,
our friends,
our lover —
are our teachers.

Pay attention and learn from them.

We know
that in this School For Love, the many
relationship tests we must undergo are for
our benefit.

Tests are not there to frustrate us, but to
help us learn so we can graduate.

Study well so you don't have to repeat
them.

We know
that love is our natural state.
We are all born innocent. But the scars
from trauma, rejection and betrayal can
distort our innate loving nature and turn
the sweet milk of kindness sour.
As we clear our hearts and minds of the
clouds of unloving thoughts, words and
actions, more of the sunlight of our true
loving self will shine through.

We know
that love's nature is to embrace.
Love seeks to
create unity . . . not separation,
promote harmony . . . not conflict,
foster cooperation . . . not competition,
extend welcome . . . not rejection.

We know
that love is able to embrace *everything,*
everything that life offers.
   Joy and sorrow.
   Pleasure and pain.
   Victory and defeat.

Every experience we have and every
person that enters our life, expands our
heart and is made more beautiful when
embraced by love.

We know
that self-love is the most basic love.
The way we offer love to ourselves
is the way we will offer love to others.
We cannot give love and we will be
unable to receive love, if we reject, judge
and detest ourself.

An empty hand can bestow no gifts.

We know
that the sweet essence of love comes from
our open-handed generosity —
overcoming our selfish tendencies and
freely giving our time, energy, attention
and material gifts to others,
rather than trying to take for ourselves.

We know
that the essence of generosity is giving
without conditions.
True love asks for nothing in return —
   no expectation of thanks,
   no call for recognition,
   no demand for anything in exchange —
just joy from giving . . .
and pleasure from seeing others receive.

We know
that we will get back what we give.
Whether generous or miserly, the love we
receive from another will mirror the love
we have given them.

We know
that love is too precious to be bought.
We cannot buy the love of others with our
money, our "niceness," our appearance,
our fame.

Love begets love.

People are drawn to the aroma of
kindness that surrounds a loving person
the way a bee is attracted to the fragrance
of a flower.

We know
that love takes courage.
When we open our heart to another,
we take the risk of being hurt.
We drop our weapons,
lay down our shield and
remove our armor.
We stand defenseless before them.

What a relief!

The armor we build around ourselves
locks in our pain. It keeps our love captive
and prevents others' love from entering.
Without armor, we are more available to
love.

We know
that our time here is limited.

One day our life and the lives of all those
we love will end.
We cannot know how or when we or they
will leave this earthly plane.
Time passes. Each moment is precious.
We should take this as a message for us to
hurry up and love deeply, love many, love
now.

Nothing is permanent.

Remembering this gives our life meaning.

We know
that love sees only the heart.

Man or woman. Rich or poor.
Straight or gay. Right wing or left.
White, black, red, yellow or brown skin —
these are only illusory differences.
Inside, every being has the same fears,
same hungers, same dreams as ourselves.

There are no strangers . . .

only family.

We know
that love heals.
Offering love from our heart plants a seed
for healing the brokenness in our own
soul and even the broken souls of lying,
power-hungry politicians, sexual
predators, hate-filled bigots and greedy
corporate heads.

We know
that love is the essential medicine that will
help to cure the illness of the world.

It is the antidote, the most potent antidote,
for the poison of hate, prejudice, greed
and injustice.

It is the explosive power of love,
not guns and bombs and missiles,
that will begin to bring peace to the world.

**We know these things to be true about
love.**

Now,
in these times of anguish and strife,
our steadfast love is needed
more than ever.

The world is in upheaval.
Old ways are dying . . .
New ways are being born.
Many are afraid of the coming change.
They fear losing their financial advantage,
losing their political control,
losing their cherished beliefs and long
held prejudices.
And they fear losing the valuable perks
that come with being rich, white and male.
They desperately try to hold on tightly to
the comfortable world they have known,
feel entitled to, and see slipping from
their grasp.

**Their fears must be addressed, with truth,
with clear boundaries and with strong
determination —**

yet also with compassion.

When dealing with those who are afraid, it is beneficial to view all as fellow humans instead of enemies. Reaching out to others with a firm, compassionate hand, rather than attacking with blame, anger and threat, can begin to soften their fear, help them loosen their grip, and open their eyes to the reality of other people's rights and needs.

This is the way to reconciliation.

It all begins within us.
A mind that is full of anger and blame,
and sees the other as an enemy,
will attack.
This cannot help but to spawn dissension.

A mind that is rooted in peace has the potential to give rise to peace in others.

This is the way of the changemaker.

In these times of transition, when chaos, hate and division reign, men who are in touch with their heart need to step forward and speak their truth.

We can do this.

Even though we may not be able to have
multitudes at our command,
we do have the ability —
with focus, determination and heart —
to grow ourselves into more loving
and lovable men.

This is enough.

Our growth-in-love is a powerful force
that cannot be contained.
It overpowers us, subdues us. We become
helplessly addicted.
Once we taste love's delicious sweetness,
we hunger for
more
and
more.

Love is infectious.
And it is highly contagious. Its nature is to
spread from person to person.

Like the ever-expanding ripples from a
rock thrown into the center of a pond,
the power of our manlove will expand,

from ourself,

    to our beloved,

      to our family,

        to our friends,

          to their friends out into the world.

In this way, even a single individual's love
can multiply and be passed on,
eventually touching thousands.

One person's expression of kindness,
one act of charity,
one unselfish action
will create widening ripples.
This will be the way that hate will fade
and love will dawn upon mankind.
Not by sermons, legislation or decree.
Lovingkindness will arise from the
generous actions of one person at a time.

Let that person be you.

An alarm is sounding
that can wake up the love
which has long been slumbering
inside you.

PERHAPS . . .

Perhaps your virile masculine self has
been fast asleep,
numbed by your addictions —
to alcohol and drugs,
to entertainment,
to possessions,
to comfort,
to sex,
to status,
to seeking the admiration of others.

Perhaps you have been mired in trying to
defend yourself against becoming aware
of your vulnerable feelings —
by engaging in false bravado,
by raging anger,
by blaming others,
by joking,
by tightlipped silence,
by burying yourself in work,
by withdrawing to the isolated safety
of your "man cave."

Perhaps you have been driven by your
fears —
of being a failure,
of not being a "real man,"
of losing control,
of not being respected,
of exposing your weakness, shame and
vulnerability, and ultimately,
your fear of unleashing your own
untested strength and freedom.

These fears, defenses and addictions are
thieves. They rob your life of meaning,
dim your vision and steal your vitality.
They enslave you.
They consume you.
They deaden you.

TIME
TO
WAKE
UP

All the while, the world,
and all those who care about you,
wait for you to wake up,
pursue your mission in life and
make use of your unique abilities
in order to bring into being the gifts
only you are destined to give.

We are men now, no longer boys.
It is time to grow up and embrace our
genuine maleness
and love like a mature man.

Love like a real person, not the phony, macho "action movie" hero image of male dominance, acclaimed by the media and promoted, through peer pressure, praise and shame, by our culture.

. . . a comic book caricature of masculinity, one who has it all together, and who allows no "fragile" human qualities to be seen.
Such a "real man" must never . . .
    show weakness,
    need help,
    fear pain,
    be indecisive,
    feel emotion, (except for
    the jolt of anger).
Such a "real man" is
    invincible — but not human.

37

Ditch that false image.
Rigidity and toughness are not the
measure of a man's strength.

Masculine strength is so much more.
   Gentleness is strength.
   Empathy is strength.
   Collaboration is strength.
   Integrity is strength.
   Love is strength.

Open your arms wide and love like a
flesh-and-blood man,
whose real potency lies in his sensitivity
to others and to himself,
his ability to express his emotions,
his compassionate generosity and
his willingness to lay down his defenses
and be vulnerable.

These, not just rigidity and toughness,
are what makes a man powerful.

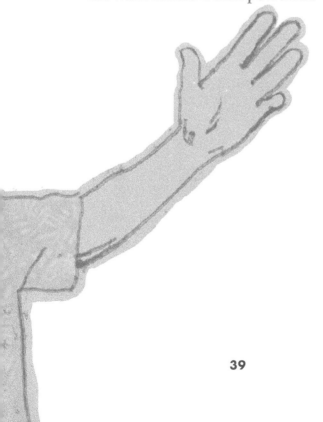

Loving in this full-hearted way is not always easy.

Authentic love takes real courage.

It takes guts for us to look into the mirror
and acknowledge that we have not been
the best loving partner, father, son, and
friend we could have been.

It takes discrimination for us to redefine
ourself and discard the idea of manhood
that requires us to have to always
compete, win, dominate and control in
order to feel we are a "real man."

Rivalry belongs on the sports field
and battlefield,
not on the playground of the heart.

It takes backbone for us to reach out and
support those who need protection,
stand up and defend ourself when we are
right, and admit responsibility and ask for
forgiveness when we are wrong.

It takes grit for us to begin to stop hiding,
start to take off our mask and consider that
we might expose our weakness, fear and
our shame in front of those whose love
and respect we seek.

It takes humility for us to surrender the isolating wall of safety, relinquish the valuable privilege that comes with being male, or white, or wealthy, and accept that we are not special and will be treated as an equal to every other person.

It takes determination for us to penetrate into our deepest values, call up our best and highest self, and show up with full masculine presence.

Roll up your sleeves.
Summon your power.

There are challenges to overcome,
battles to be fought.

OOGA
BOOGA

Fearsome dragons wait to be slain —
your inner dragons —
Anger. Fear. Laziness. Arrogance.
Confusion. Dispair. Selfishness.
Apathy.

The weapons in your arsenal are lethal
dragon killers —
Gentleness defeats anger.
Courage neutralizes fear.
Disipline conquers laziness.
Humility subdues arrogance.
Clarity dispels confusion.
Hope quells dispair.
Generosity destroys selfishness.
Passion overcomes apathy.

These weapons are effective,
but not at your instant command.
It will take you time and effort to develop
them.

Take the time . . .
Make the effort.

You will need this powerful artillery,
because these dragons you must slay
are cunning and dangerous.

They are so treacherous because they lurk
close by . . .

. . . they
hide
within
your
own
mind.

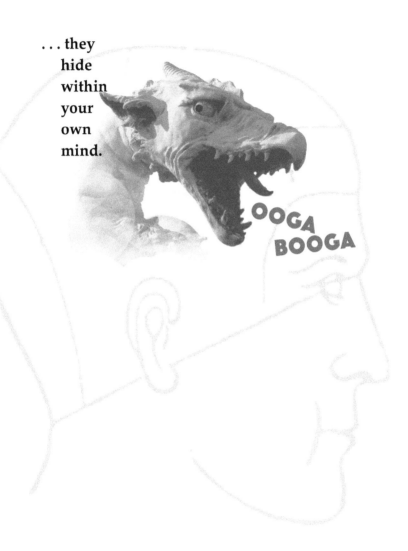

OOGA
BOOGA

Quiet your mind in order to clear
its disruptive chatter.

Sit alone in silence. Rest in the peace of
your own Being.

With a quiet mind you will be able to hear
the voice of your truth.

As if you are a hunter in the woods . . .
freeze . . .
track the teeming thoughts swirling in
your head . . .

and ignore the chatter.

Instead, pursue that solid, muted
soul-voice in the stillness,
a voice that doesn't shout, but whispers
in your ear with boundless integrity,
heartfelt kindness and
unwavering truth.

Love dwells in that stillness.

Amplify that pure inner voice so you can
hear, learn from it, and grow soul-deep.

Amplify so that the soul's profound
message of love and hope is broadcast far
and wide for everyone to receive
and be uplifted.

Don't try to go it alone.

Be one strand that combines with others
to contribute to the strength of a mighty
cable.

Real change can only happen when good
people, with shared vision, join together.

A single, isolated voice can easily be
ignored . . . but many voices in unison
will be heard and cannot be silenced.

Join with other men of good will,
as a man among men, as a member in a
community of men, who together can
occupy a space where they can feel safe
  to be themselves,
    to share and
     debate and
       play and
        confess and
         laugh and
            angrily HOWL against man's
            inhumanity.

Join with other men to celebrate your
brotherhood — that kinship you share
with all other males.

But don't just gab about cars and sports,
money and politics.
Speak to each other from your heart and
from your gut,
not just from your head.
Share with your brothers about
what you love,
what you fear,
what you want,
what has wounded you,
what holds joy and meaning for you.
Your openness with them will invite their
openness and create a bond of truth and
brotherhood.

No roles, no masks, no bullshit.
You will meet in a place of authentic self.

Sharing from our hearts will heal us.

Secrets we withhold out of fear or shame will fester and sicken us.

The time is ripe.
The winds of change are blowing.

Women have bravely risen up and have
been speaking out.

The voices of strong women who refuse
to be bullied and dominated by men are
being heard and are making a difference.

Their righteous anger, their truth and their
courage is reverberating throughout the
world.

It's men's turn now to speak.

By joining together, circles of purpose-driven men, full with integrity and heart, can help change the downward trajectory we are all headed as a society and as a species.

Our bold male presence is needed.

Time to stop choking on our
dissatisfaction and frustration.
Time to put an end to our uncomfortable
silence.
Time to lift our voice with other men and
form a "coalition of conscience" to expose
those who worship at the altar of money
and power, who don't know the meaning
of the word, "enough" and who plunder to
obtain immediate profit for
themselves, without a care for
the generations of children
and their children's children,
who will suffer tomorrow
because of these men's
greed of today.

We need to direct our caring attention to
the young. Children are of the future.
They will be living in a world that present
generations are building for them
right now.

We cannot let them down by standing
around while their future is being stolen
piece by piece.

Take action so that we will leave them a
legacy they will appreciate and a future
we will feel proud of having helped to
create for them.

 Children's tender hearts are hungry now
for our care and for that special kind of
masculine love only a man is able to give.

Let us focus our manlove on the sons.

Boys everywhere are lacking inspiring models of manhood they can look up to.

You be that model.

They have need for good men, men with moral fiber, who can guide them on their path.

You be that guide.

Show them — by your example — what a loving father, partner, son, and friend is like.

Boys become good men by having a good man in their life.

Bless the daughters with your attention.

Show them — by your example — what a good man is, what a good man does, how a good man acts around women.

Your respectful behavior toward women will be a model for how she will want to be treated by the men in her life when she grows up.

In future relationships she forms, she will not be content with anything less than the quality of character you had shown her when she was young.

Be her coach, be her cheerleader.
Praise her and encourage her to aim high,
break through glass ceilings and grow
beyond the artificial barriers our society
puts in her way.

Inspire her to develop her gifts and become the finest human being she can be.

There is no Operator's Manual for
becoming a good father or mentor of
young people.
We learned by being the son of our
own father.

Was he the loving father you wanted him
to be or
was he distant?
Was he violent?
Did he judge you?
Compete with you?
Was he too busy to spend quality time
with you?

You don't have to follow in your father's footsteps.

Forgive him for being the imperfect dad he was.

And *you* be the father you wanted *him* to be.

Life continually presents us with challenging people, places and situations that require our assertive intervention. Withdrawing into our shell like a turtle is not an option.

There is more to our life than filling our belly or cheering for our favorite team.

It's time to get off our butts. Unplug the computer. Put down the phone. Switch off the TV.

Don't just complain. You are not helpless.
In order to bring more peace and justice
into the world . . .
do something . . . say something.

Hoping for change is not enough.

Take firm but loving action.
Bring your unselfish concern and
caring feelings out into the world.

YOU CAN. . .

 — Honor and respect women. Women are not property. Women are not just a body, a trophy or an object in a game you win by "scoring."

Listen to them.
Value their feminine wisdom.
Learn from them.
Openly champion their equality and fair treatment.

Women know things we can't understand.

☞ — Show keen interest in what your local schools are teaching children about gender inequality, bullying, racial prejudice and,
yes,
about love.

☞ — Teach your children to be kind and respectful to all, to be honest and industrious and to take responsibility for their behavior.

There is no better way to teach them than by being a living model for what you want them to learn.

YOU CAN...

— Speak out to demand that those who
hold power and serve you in government,
business, law enforcement and media,
do so with the intention for integrity and
compassion, rather than for manipulation
and profit.

Hold them to account if they fail to do so.

— Stand up in support of those whose
power is being diluted and whose voice
is being suppressed — the poor, the aged,
minorities, women, gays and children.

☞ — Contribute your time and resources to support causes and organizations that you feel strongly about.

☞ — Meet in groups and inspire each other.

☞ — Keep informed of what is happening in the world.

☞ — Write to your congressperson and editor of your local newspaper.

☞ — Be a presence on social media networks.

☞ — Express your desire with your vote.

☞ — Don't stand on the sidelines. Come out and march arm-in-arm with like-minded brothers and sisters.

YOU CAN. . .

— Make the things you value known in everyday conversation with your buddies.
Your truth and passion can help ignite their passion.

— Take issue when you hear people make jokes or put down other's race, gender, religious beliefs or sexual orientation. Standing up in public for your values is a powerful, loving act.

— Have the courage to call out acts of unkindness when you see them occur.
If you do not protest unloving actions of others, your silence can be seen as approval and your inaction can promote more unkindness.

— Be sensitive to the feelings of those with whom you disagree.
Do not provoke, ridicule or taunt them. Their feelings matter.

— Don't numb yourself to your feelings of compassion that naturally arise when you are confronted with the suffering of others.

When you look into their eyes . . . see yourself.

☞ — Treat the fellow creatures that share our Earth as family. Those living beings that crawl on the land, fly in the air and swim in the sea are our cousins.
They need us to speak for them.

☞ — Speak out to honor our precious Earth as a living being. She needs our protection. Greedy, uncaring humans right now are causing permanent insult to her ground, air and water.

Are we to stand mute as they line their pockets while destroying our home?
Speak out.

☞ — Have compassion for those whose lack of love is causing damage and hardship in the world. Their destructive actions are the result of their own ignorance, their own suffering. They are bringing about misery to themselves as well as to others.

While always making sure that steps are taken to repair the damage they have caused and minimize the harm they are creating, we must hold them legally accountable and morally answerable for their misdeeds.

73

Compassion does not mean being passive.
Our having compassion for those who do
evil should not relieve them from being
punished for what they have done.
Punishment changes behavior.

But we shouldn't stew in anger or harbor
hate for them. And we shouldn't wish
them pain.
If we hate or seek revenge, we become
                              them.

You can do all these things, as they are clearly beneficial actions to take.
But really, the most effective way to call forth goodness, harmony and love into the world and into your life is to actively do whatever you can to become a more loving person.

Love elicits love.
People respond with love to the love they are given

So, if you want to bring more love into your life . . . be the change you want to see.
Be more loving.

If you want to bring more love into the world . . . don't lecture, don't threaten, don't shame . . .
Be more loving.

And if you want to be more loving . . .
practice love.

Practicing love is simple. Ask yourself the question, "Will the words I am about to speak, the actions I am about to take, serve to bring more love and harmony, or will my words and actions bring more distance?"

And then, follow the answer and do the loving thing . . . and again, do the loving thing.

If you are still uncertain as to what is the loving thing, employ the Golden Rule. You'll sense what's right for others by looking inside and feeling what's right for you.

PRACTICE

Don't start your love practice off by trying to love your enemies or those engaging in evil. Begin by practicing love and acceptance for the person closest to you . . . yourself.

Over and over, practice letting go of constant self-criticism, striving for perfection, comparing yourself to others. When these toxic thoughts arise, look within and recognize the incomparable miracle you are.

Then, turn your lovelight to the people around you. Practice being more loving with your family, friends and neighbors. The circle of those closest to you is where the tire meets the road.

This is the crucible where the most opportunities to practice love will arise. This is where you can directly experience the effects of your loving actions. And this is where love has the most *practice!* meaning for you.

Once you become more established in love for self and for those close to you, it will be far easier to expand your love out into the world, to the strangers who wander in and out of your life.

Then comes the real test . . . the difficult but necessary task of extending kindness and forgiveness for those who hurt you or whose actions are hurting others. PRACTICE

Cultivating an open heart for these people is essential work that will help free you from the trap of anger and blame.

Without taking this challenging step, you cannot fully manifest your love.

Practice

There are many ways for us to actively cultivate love in our life and the lives of others.

We can manifest love-in-action by . . .

— being gentle and kind to ourselves and taking meticulous loving care of our precious body, mind and spirit.

— being fully present with our loved ones, intent in our listening, sensitive to their needs, surrounding them with loving concern and fierce, protective, warrior devotion.

— bringing the light of our humor, joy, creativity, imagination, spontaneity, excitement and childlike playfulness into every aspect of our life and the lives of others.

— celebrating our natural innocence. Let's not take our role as a protector, "fixer" and breadwinner so seriously that we forget to care for the pure, sweet child that resides within us.

— never being content to lay back and stagnate, but to use our precious time and energy for taking in new information and new experiences. In this way we continually challenge ourselves to mature and evolve intellectually, emotionally and spiritually.

Growth and learning never ends.

— being willing to allow ourselves to
be known. It takes courage to share ourselves truthfully, openly . . . not just the
admirable parts that we want others to see,
but also the ugly, unloved parts we try to
hide.

Leave nothing out. The more of ourselves
we share, the more of us is available to be
loved.

— having an *attitude of gratitude*. We
shouldn't neglect counting our blessings
and keeping in mind the plight of those
who are less fortunate than ourselves.
Being grateful for the abundance and
good people in our life invites more
goodness.

— spending as much time as we can with uplifting, loving people. They inspire us. But those who have yet to develop a loving heart can deter us and bring us down.

The company we keep is a powerful influence on who we become.

— having patience, for ourselves, for others and for the situations we encounter. Enduring temporary discomfort, letting go of trying to force or control, allowing things to unfold naturally, these are the properties of a patient mind.

Patience is an essential ingredient for harmony and love.

— freely expressing our love and appreciation for others through our words, our touch, our presence, our kindness. Everyone we care about needs to know they are loved by us.

— receiving others through listening, observing, sensing. We should make the effort to diligently try to decipher the true feelings that lay behind their words and actions. Our conscious attention to others is healing and is the most profound way to communicate.

Receiving another person is an act of love.

— looking for and emphasizing the positive in people. Focusing on the positive inspires and motivates. Focusing too much on what is wrong can discourage and can invite more negativity.

— judging others less and being more accepting and flexible.

Nobody is perfect, including ourselves. It is foolish to expect or demand that people think, look, speak and act the way we want them to. Accepting those who differ from us opens the door to appreciate another person's world.

Judging slams the door shut.

— being more open to forgive. The past is over and cannot be undone. Holding on to festering anger and resentment is painful. Forgiveness begins the process of releasing both the "offender" and ourselves from the prison of blame, and helps restore balance and equanimity.

Offering forgiveness benefits us as well as them.

— remembering that we are more than body, mind and personalities.
We are all sacred souls, all composed of the same divine stuff.
No soul is better or worse, higher or lower, more or less deserving of kindness than another soul.

— understanding that human dignity is precious. Each and every person needs to be treated with respect, no matter who they are or what they do.

— finding ultimate value in our inner self — who we are, rather than externals, like things we own, how much we know and what we do and have done.
Power, prestige and possessions won't guarantee a happy life. Fulfillment comes from living with passion, integrity, generosity and devotion.

— being in awe of the majesty and unfathomable mystery of nature and of the cosmos.
Look upon the face of a child.
Hold a flower in your hand.
Go outside at night and gaze up at the stars.
And contemplate the miracle of you.

That which is sacred often hides in ordinary places.

Expressing love-in-action is no big deal.
Great love is rarely expressed by
performing magnificent gestures.
No need to be a Mother Teresa.
Great love can be found in small kind-
nesses. . . like holding the door open for
the next person, lowering our headlights
for oncoming cars, aiding an elder
crossing the street, putting the toilet seat
down for the ladies.

Small actions, but done with a big heart.

Every act, large or small, can be an expression of our deepest values.

GREAT
LOVE CAN
BE FOUND
IN SMALL
KIND-
NESSES.

Great love begins within us.
In order to manifest great love we need to aspire to greatness of heart.

We develop a loving heart when we seek to cultivate those ideal qualities of character in ourselves that define an honorable man — virtuous qualities, like
integrity,
kindness,
authenticity,
trustworthiness,
generosity,
honesty,
gratitude,
empathy,
receptivity,
patience,
forgiveness,
joy.

These are all qualities that make up the essence of a loving person.

Virtues are the basic building blocks that comprise the foundation of any loving relationship. They create good and avoid harm.

Without virtue, real love cannot exist because virtuous behavior gives rise to one of the most fundamental ingredients of all human connection . . . trust.

We develop trust for those who are trust-worthy.

Virtues are what makes us lovable . . .
able to be desired and loved by others
                    and
They are what makes us love-able . . .
able to offer love and care to others.

Virtue is expressed through the habitual ways that we behave.

Just like any other habit or skill, such as learning to play piano or shoot basketballs, virtuous actions are strengthened by practice.

As we repeatedly practice and perfect them, and also work to eliminate unvirtuous actions, virtue becomes our habit.

We become a skilled lover.

Over time, we will receive the fruits of those virtuous actions — happiness, inner peace, harmonious relationships, the satisfaction of knowing we have made a difference and the gratification of having people trust and respect us for being an honorable person.

Great love lives as potential within you.
It waits for you to claim it.
Lay claim by choosing love.
The way of choosing love is so simple, so
powerful . . . but not so easy.

Choose love by making a conscious
decision to turn away from unloving
thoughts, words and actions.

When dark thoughts of blame, hate, greed,
jealousy and retaliation first begin to arise
in your mind, do not act on them.
Be aware of them . . .
acknowledge them . . .
but then turn away.

Gently turn your focus toward the light of
kind thoughts,
kind words,
kind, beneficial,
generous loving actions.

It's that simple.

Choose love.

To take loving action — or not —
is a choice you commit to make and
remake moment by moment.

Each day,
   all day,
      every day,
with everyone who crosses your path,
be they
friend or stranger,
   ally or adversary,
      prince or pauper,
         saint or sinner —
commit to put in the effort to choose love.

CHOOSE LOVE
CHOOSE LOVE CHOOSE LOVE CHOOSE LOVE
CHOOSE LOVE CHOOSE LOVE CHOOSE LOVE

CHOOSE TO BE KIND

Commit to choose to be kind
for the sake of love,
not for the sake of your ego.

Perform your loving actions stealthily,
when
nobody
is
looking.

Commit to inhabit your heart when you are stressed and upset. When the fierce winds of disturbed emotions are blowing, focus your attention on the space in the center of your chest.
Breathe into that space.

Feel from your heart.

Listen from your heart.

Speak from your heart.

Act from your heart.

Your heart is your calm, safe harbor. Peace will take hold and love will flow more freely when your awareness is centered in your heart.

Commit to choose love even if others try
to harm you, belittle you, manipulate you,
frustrate you.
In the midst of their abuse . . . even while
standing up strong for what is right and
just . . . commit again and again to choose
to take the loving path.

This is your test.
Avoiding adversity will weaken you.
Lovingly confronting the people and
things you find difficult to love will help
you discover your strength and resilience.

**When you encounter challenges, your love
will be unbreakable.**

Commit over the long-haul to realizing the
loving and lovable man that you are.

This is the work of a lifetime . . .
a marathon, not a sprint.

There will be hills and there will be
valleys. You may become frustrated and
exhausted and want to quit. Don't!
The rewards for learning to live a
love-centered life are beyond value.

And when you occasionally fail in your
noble practice of dispersing loving kindness to all, and fall prey to angry, harmful
thoughts and hurtful actions . . .
love yourself anyway.
Love yourself for trying.
You are not the perfect man.
You are not a saint.
You are a flawed person, just like
everyone else.
Love yourself for being human and appreciate yourself for making the effort.

Then lift yourself up, dust yourself off,
and again . . .

choose love.

Time after time, when you choose love,
choose love, choose love . . .
love will choose you.

Everything you think, say and do will
radiate from your love . . .

because you are love.

In time, the power of your loving heart
will seep from every pore.
You will have become a loving presence.
Your presence will be a guiding light,
an inspiration for all those who see, hear
and know you.

You will have embodied the stature of
  a man of heart,
    a man of conscience,
      a safe and trustworthy partner,
        and a loving and lovable man.

Your strong arms, wise voice and loving
presence will be manifest.
When you step forward and assume
authority and address the wrongs you see
happening around you, you will be a force
for good.
Your powerful presence and incorruptible
masculine love will help transform your
home, your family, your world into a
kinder, safer place.

Your strength will be
a sanctuary for the
flowering of love.

MEN.
Men of good will . . .
Come awake.
Come alive.
Come home to love.

The world is in turmoil.
Forces of greed and hate are assembling
and eagerly preparing to take control.

They will succeed if none resist.

Now you are called.
Listen . . . Hear.
Answer the call from your heart.

Time is precious.
Don't waver.
Don't delay.
Don't wait for others.
Weigh the options.
Know the consequences.

Make the choice.

Choose truth. Choose love.

BECOME A WARRIOR FOR KINDNESS.

RICHARD MATZKIN, MA, counts as his greatest accomplishment his four-decade loving marriage to his wife, Alice.

He was director of a program for men who were violent towards their partners, program director at a psychiatric hospital and had been active in men's work, both as a leader and participant. He is an accomplished sculptor and jazz drummer.

His books, LOVING PROMISES: *The Master Class For Creating Magnificent Relationship*, and THE ART OF AGING: *Celebrating The Authentic Aging Self* (co-authored with Alice Matzkin), have won multiple book awards. His latest book, titled ManKINDness: *How A Man Can Become A More Loving And Lovable Partner*, is due to be published late 2020.

matzkinstudio.com

RILEY K. SMITH, MA, MFT, is an artist and a psychotherapist. His first career was illustrating and designing ads and books. In 1976 he became a psychotherapist and did both careers until 1987 when he began devoting full time to psychotherapy, as Clinical Director at an out-patient drug rehab program, training therapists and also in private practice treating adults and couples. In 2004 he joined the faculty of the Integrative Body Psychotherapy Central Institute in Santa Monica teaching body-mind psychotherapy.

Riley is semi-retired and lives with his beloved wife, Rhoda Pregerson, MA, MFT, in West Los Angeles.

He is co-author of HOW TO BE A COUPLE AND STILL BE FREE and TRUE PARTNERS, *A Work-book for Building a Lasting Intimate Relationship.* His most recent book is ONE TRUTH THAT CHANGES EVERYTHING.

Richard and Riley are close friends and were active together in the Men's Movement and co-led men's therapy groups in Los Angeles.

CPSIA information can be obtained
at www.ICGtesting.com
Printed in the USA
BVHW061044310821
615257BV00003B/3